How to say Hello to a Dog

An A-Z Guide to dogs for children ...and adults

Tim Liddiard

Introduction

Whether you own a dog now or are thinking of owning a dog in the future, it's never too late to teach children the correct way to interact with dogs and other animals. This book is designed to offer an insight into dog behaviour and how children can play a positive part in their life.

Following these guidelines will not only keep children safer, but also offer your dogs a more relaxed and enriched environment.

This book is designed to be read with an adult. There are of course pictures, supported by a little rhyming caption that might be fun to say or sing out loud. There is also an additional section for adults to explain to children, with supporting fun facts, plus interesting and useful information.

The information contained within these pages is basic and should only be used as a guide. If you are experiencing complications with your dog, a professional dog behaviourist should be sought. Remember, anyone working with dogs should only employ positive reinforcement training techniques, rather than aversive dominance-based ones.

If I were to choose one letter it would be P; P for Patience, Praise and Positive. Dogs, like children and adults, need to grow and learn, and like us, they are sure to make some mistakes. But with lots of patience, heaps of praise when they get something right, and a positive reward-based approach to their training and development, we can help guide them on their way to a happy and fulfilled life with us.

Enjoy sharing your life, full of unconditional love.

Best wishes

Tim

Did you know:

When you adopt someone, you invite them to be part of your family and live with you forever.

There are thousands of dogs in rescue kennels who are waiting for new homes.

Never purchase a dog from unknown sources on the internet. Instead visit your local rescue charity and discuss your needs with their staff.

A a

A is for Adopt

Though they wait in a kennel afraid and alone

They know that in time

They'll soon find a new forever home.

Did you know:

Bones can be a great way to keep a dog entertained. It is important however that they are supervised and that are only given bones recommended by a reputable supplier. They should never be given left over bones from your plate, especially chicken bones, as these can easily splinter and cause serious harm to your dog.

Children should NEVER approach a dog who is eating.

B b is for Bone

A big beautiful bone to munch and to chew

At any time of day

Keeps me busy with something to do.

Did you know:

A cuddle can be a lovely thing to have, but remember that not everyone will enjoy a cuddle all of the time. Rescue dogs can sometimes take a long time before they feel ready to give cuddles and sometimes, they never do. Older dogs may feel pain in their joints and so will not want cuddles.

Always wait for your dog to ask for a cuddle before trying to give one.

Please discourage children from trying to cuddle their dogs like they do their teddy bears.

C c is for Cuddle

A cuddle can be nice if it's a cuddle we need

But be sure first to ask us

Or we may just struggle to be free.

Did you know:

Some dogs like to dig holes. Some because they like to bury things and some because they like to dig holes. Perhaps because they are bored and need something to do, or perhaps because they are stressed and it helps them to cope.

If you have a dog who likes to dig, consider giving them a sand pit to dig in. You can encourage them by hiding treats or toys in there and make it a fun game.

This will be great for them and it may save your lawn.

D d

is for Dig

Digging in dirt is a fun thing to do

I can make a great big hole

To bury a bone or a chew.

Did you know:

It is extremely important that no one, especially children, tries to forcibly take something away from a dog. Instead offer them something of value to exchange it for. Most will exchange for something tasty such as cheese, hot dogs etc.

Remember that you do not need to prove that you are 'Top Dog' or 'Alpha', it's completely unnecessary. Dogs are like children, they are not trying to dominate you, they might just try it on sometimes, a bit like children.

If your dog shows signs of possession it is not a challenge to you.

Even if a dog has never shown signs of possession before, if people keep taking things away from them, then they may start resource guarding. Better safe than sorry, always exchange and always ask an adult.

E e

is for Exchange

If I steal your favourite teddy or a toy then please

Ask an adult to help you exchange your stuff

I may swap for a little hot dog or some really smelly cheese.

Did you know:

It is very important that your dog has a healthy diet. That means that they are given the right type and amount of food. If they are given too much food, they can become overweight and very unwell. This means that food should be weighed or measured and the correct amount given. Treats can be given but should be accounted for, therefore if children have given treats, they need to let adults know how many.

Children must remember that some foods are poisonous to dogs, especially chocolate.

If you have a dog who has a good food motivation, stop feeding it in a bowl. You are missing out on an excellent opportunity to give your dog some fantastic enrichment. Put their food in a food toy such as a Kong, or at least scatter their food on the kitchen floor. It will keep them busy, slow down their eating and keep them entertained. It's easy for you and great for them.

F

is for food

f

My favourite time is breakfast, lunch and dinner time

I am more than happy to help you eat your food

Right after I've eaten mine.

Did you know:

When a dog growls they are trying to communicate. It is vitally important that we listen to them and never discourage them from trying to communicate what is upsetting them.

Your dog may be frightened of other dogs, strangers, cars, loud noises, someone stealing its food, stealing its possessions, coming too close, approaching its bed, or any number of things. If your dog growls you need to listen and never tell it off for demonstrating that it is unhappy.

For example: if you are frightened of spiders, shouting at you will not change that, neither will it help if people keep bringing you spiders.

As a word of warning, if a dog is constantly ignored when it growls over something, that dog will eventually stop growling ...and just bite instead.

G g is for growl

If at times I growl it might be because I'm scared

Please don't tell me off or shout

I don't speak human but if you listen, dog is a
language we can share.

Did you know:

If you have a pet dog, you have decided to add another member to your family. Dogs are sociable creatures like us and although some may be more independent than others, they all want to be part of a family. Therefore, if you have a pet dog, especially a rescue dog, that dog should spend its time indoors with you and sleep indoors as part of the family.

Outside kennels may be ok for short periods, but while you are at home and at night, your pet dog would be happier indoors with you.

H is for home

You adopted me to your family and invited me into your home

I love my people and don't want to sleep in a kennel all alone.

Did you know:

Some breeds of dogs are considered more intelligent than others, these are generally referred to as working dogs. They have the ability and desire to learn and prefer to be kept very busy. They are not generally considered ideal for first time owners or for people with busy lives that cannot include their dogs in their busy lifestyle.

It is important to know that an intelligent dog without a purpose in its life, is likely to become bored and may display unwanted behaviours such as howling or destroying things. These types of dogs need to be kept busy.

It is important therefore to research which breed suits your lifestyle, before adopting.

I i is for intelligent

Home work:

Some dogs help us see and others help us hear

Some dogs like to pull a sledge whilst others keep us free from fear.

Did you know:

Some dogs are quite adept at jumping. They might like to jump up to say hello to people, others like to explore and so will jump fences to escape. Fences should be high enough to stop your dog from escaping if that is something it might do. It is recommended that on average, fences should be 6ft high before they would be considered secure. However, there are some determined dogs who can still escape these.

If you have a dog who is energetic and loves to run and jump, perhaps try some agility or flyball, it may be the best thing your dog has ever done. Contact your local clubs for more information.

J 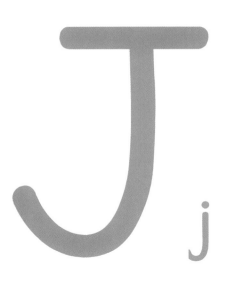 is for Jump

j

I can jump very high for the ball in the garden, the beach or the park

I can jump with a splosh and a splash, in a puddle, the sea or a lake

Can I jump on your lap for a cuddle, if I'm worried and afraid of the dark?

Did you know:

Some dogs like to lick you and we tend to call this a kiss. They may be licking you for affection, to taste you or it may have become a learnt behaviour that they employ because it gives them attention. Some people don't like to be 'kissed' by dogs and that is fine, but a 'kiss' on the cheek from a healthy dog isn't normally going to do you any harm.

If you don't want kisses offer to do something else with your dog, such as play a game.

K

k

What's better than TV, what's better than chocolate and crisps,

What's better than anything else, what could possibly be better than this?

The best thing of all is the love of your dog, complete with a big sloppy kiss.

Did you know:

The World's tallest dog was a Great Dane who measured a whopping 44 inches (111cm) compared to the World's smallest dog, a Chihuahua, who stood less than 4 inches. (10cm) How tall are you?

If a Great Dane stands on its back legs it can stand over seven feet tall! That's taller than most adults.

An adult Great Dane can weigh 120 lbs (54kgs / 8.5 stone). An adult Chihuahua can weigh 3-6 lbs. How much do you weigh?

L is for Little and Large

L l

Your dog might be big,
they might be small

They might be short,
they might be tall

Whether they fit in
your pocket or are
bigger than you

No matter their size,
their love for us is true.

Did you know:

Some dogs just love to cover themselves in mud and other stinky substances. This is probably a genetic throwback to a time where they may have wished to mask their own scent. Or maybe they just like to get messy.

Make sure bath times are a positive experience with lots of rewards throughout for tolerating, followed by a warm fluffy towel to dry them off, and something tasty to take to their bed afterwards. Remember to only use shampoo for dogs, not humans.

M m is for Mud

I love to roll in mud and love to jump in puddles

Now, who wants to be the first to give me a big squishy cuddle?

Did you know:

A dog's sense of smell is 100,000 times better than ours!

Dogs have been known to smell something 40 feet underground or in 80 feet of water, and in the right conditions could smell something a mile away! Dogs can also breathe in and out at exactly the same time.

The dogs with the best noses are the Hound dogs and other breeds with longer noses. The worst are the short nose breeds such as Bulldogs, French bulldogs and pugs.

N n is for Nose

I have a shiny wet nose that can breathe and can smell

Your sausages in the fridge or a man down a well

So clever is my nose, much better than yours you see

I can smell underground or far out to sea.

Did you know:

Despite the old saying, you can still teach an old dog new tricks.

In rescue shelters the older dogs nearly always take the longest to rehome. They can make fantastic pets as they have often already learnt how to be sociable, are house trained and unlike youngsters will not be so physically demanding. They make the most fantastic companion dogs.

They will love you forever, for giving them their final forever home.

Please remember that like people, they will feel the cold more the older they get, and like us, their joints will hurt more. It is important that we are sensitive to this.

O₀ is for Old

I may creak and groan when I move

I may be old and slow and like to sleep all the time

But I still love to snuggle as long as you're gentle

And I am happy and content that you're mine.

Did you know:

Play forms a very important part of your dog's training, enrichment and development. Play is also a great way to relieve boredom and stress in dogs. It is also great to help you bond with your dog.

Play with other dogs is how puppies learn social skills. But other dogs aren't always available, and besides your dog wants your attention so you have to be involved. Therefore, you need to make sure you set some time aside for some playtime with your dog.

Play can and should, involve a mixture of both physical activities such as ball play in the garden or park, agility, Fly-ball etc. along with mental activities such as training indoors, food puzzles, food toys, snuffle mats, search games and a whole lot more. You'll have a more content dog who will love you for it.

For more ideas simply do a search for' mental enrichment for dogs' on the internet.

P p is for Play

I love to play at home, I love to play in the park

Let's go chase a tennis ball, until it gets dark.

Did you know:

Like some people, many dogs have a fear of loud noises. Here are a few examples: fireworks, thunder, shouting and screaming, cars, motorbikes and lorries, balloons popping, smoke alarms, guns firing, the list could go on.

It is important that owners of these types of dogs are sensitive to this and try to help, by ensuring that their dogs are not exposed needlessly to such noises. Sometimes, unfortunately, Firework Night, for example, it is unavoidable. On such occasions, ensure your dog is kept inside with curtains and windows closed and play music or put the TV on. If your dog wants to hide, let it.

If you are having a party at home and you have a sensitive dog, then consider sending them to a family member or friend's home, where they can have some peace and quiet. If that isn't possible then perhaps, they could have access to a room away from all of the noise.

Q

q

is for Quiet

I get worried by the thunder, I get worried by the lightening

I don't like it when people shout and find fireworks quite frightening

Balloons popping and noisy cars might make me jump inside

When things get scary, all I can do is find somewhere safe to hide.

Did you know:

It is a little-known fact, that many dogs enjoy being read to. They enjoy the sound of your voice and often find the whole experience relaxing.

The next time you would like your dog to settle, try reading them a story, they won't mind what you choose.

When children are of reading age, this is something you can encourage them to do as well.

R r is for Read

Tell me a story, I don't mind what it's your choice

I'll sit with you anywhere, I just want to hear your voice.

Did you know:

That most dogs can sleep more than half of their life; 14-16 hours a day.

It is really, really important that children are taught to never wake a dog up, as this is when the majority of dog bites with children occur. (60%)

Better still, make your dog's bed a 'no go' area for anyone other than your dog.

Make sure your dog's bed is in a quiet corner of a room away from heavy footfall.

If you want to crate train your dog, ensure that it is a positive experience and that they are free to come and go.

S is for Sleep

I like to sleep in the night, I like to sleep in the day

I can sleep in my bed, or yours, or the sofa if that's ok

I don't mind where I sleep, as long as I can get quite comfy

But whatever you do, don't wake me up or I might get really grumpy.

Did you know:

The most important thing you can do when taking on a dog, especially a rescue dog, is to build trust. This can take time and an awful lot of love and patience. For some dogs this means that you and your family will need to take things very slowly.

This can start with a simple hello. Never allow children to approach an unknown dog without first seeking permission. Especially, do not allow them to run towards a dog. Do not lean over a dog and don't try to pat it on top of its head. Instead they should allow the dog to approach them and when ready, offer slowly, one hand for them to sniff. For especially small dogs, crouching down is often better. If the dog is relaxed after this a gentle stroke on the chest may be acceptable.

Most importantly, do not rush things. This can sometimes take days or weeks. For some dogs who are nervous of new people, precautions should be put into place if you have visitors to the home. Consider 'baby gates' to keep areas segregated, and always ask visitors to sit and ignore your dog. Only introduce your dog if you are confident to do so and the dog is in a calm state. Allowing your dog to investigate new people when it's ready to and not before, without strangers putting pressure on it by making eye contact or speaking to it, will increase your dog's chances of relaxing. Never allow other people's children to try and interact with a nervous dog.

I cannot stress enough that children should not manhandle or play rough with dogs, sit on them, pull their ears or tails. Even the most relaxed dog would find this annoying.

T is for Trust

T t

Trust is a thing that is earnt with time

Show me that you love me and your love is mine

And I will love you and my trust in you will shine.

Did you know:

We all wish we were Dr Doolittle and could speak to the animals. Unfortunately, the best we can do is try and learn their body language, something by the way that dogs are much better at doing than we are.

Remember that most of your words mean very little to your dog, your own body language and tone will say much more. Remember that often a dog's body language can be very subtle and it is the combination of the whole body that gives the best indication to how the dog is feeling., not just one part of the body. For example; a wagging tail does not necessarily mean that your dog is happy. There are different types of 'wags' and some of them mean highly stressed, aroused, excited and of course happy. Look to what the rest of the body is doing, the ears, eyes, tongue. How about the posture, what noises if any is your dog making? There is a lot of information out there available to you and it is worth spending time getting to know what your dog is saying.

Although Dogs do not speak human, it is worth taking the time to teach your dog some key words through positive reward-based training. This will help your dog to understand some of what you are asking it. All of this comes with time and patience, and consistent training. It is important that the whole family are following the same training structure or your dog will be confused and not understand what is expected of it.

U is for Understand

Uu

Do you speak any dog? Because I don't speak Human you see

But I can tell that you love me even when I'm not sure what you mean

And I'm grateful that you're patient and take time to help me.

Did you know:

Hopefully your trips to the vets will be minimal, and for nothing more than your dog's annual vaccination booster. It is worth getting your dog used to going to the vets, to become familiar with the look, smell and noise of the place. This will hopefully help when the time comes for a necessary visit.

Consider taking them at a quiet time and just sitting in the waiting room for a few minutes, and then rewarding them for a job well done. This will then make a trip to the vets a positive experience, not a traumatic one.

Wherever possible please try to insure your dog, just in case there's an emergency, and remember you must microchip your dog and they must wear a collar with a tag, in a public place.

V is for Vet

When it's time to see the doggie doctor

A person called a vet

We know that they'll look after us

Because they all love our Pets.

Did you know:

Daily exercise for most dogs forms an important part of their life and offers daily enrichment. It's not only that exercise is good for all of us, but it offers the opportunity for your dog to experience new things. Allowing dogs to sniff will fill their brains with information, which counts towards part of their daily enrichment.

If you have a puppy, it is crucial to socialise them as soon as possible. Ideally try to make sure they are only meeting well behaved dogs. Walk on a relaxed lead and consider a harness. Work on their recall before letting them off lead. Although children can walk dogs, if they can manage them, they cannot legally be responsible for their actions so should always be supervised.

If your dog is frightened of other dogs, walk them in quiet areas away from dogs. Continually exposing them to situations that cause them to become stressed, will not improve their behaviour.

Please remember that in a public place your dog must always be under your control. If your dog has no recall then keep it on a long line or lead. If your dog is uncomfortable around other dogs keep it on a lead. If your dog is friendly with dogs, but can be rude, do not allow it to run up to unknown dogs in the park. Other people's dogs may be very uncomfortable or frightened around other dogs.

W w is for Walk

Our walks are important, it's more than just stretching legs

More important than muddy paws and muddy shoes

It allows us to sniff and fill our brains with lots of news.

Did you know:

It is a well-known fact that many dogs love to chew things. Whilst that might be unfortunate if they destroy your slippers, it becomes a rather more serious problem if they also ingest what they're chewing. Although this is common in puppies, adult dogs can also do this.

If you have a dog that eats 'anything', make sure your family are picking things up from the floor, especially children and their toys. Not only might your children lose a favourite toy, your dog might end up in the vets for an x-ray. A potentially dangerous and expensive outcome.

It is worth noting that wherever possible insuring your dog will give you peace of mind, should anything unforeseen arise.

X x is for X-ray

An x-ray is very clever, it's like a camera you see

A clever camera your vet might use to see what's inside my belly.

Did you know:

A puppy's natural behaviour is to chew, make sure valuables are kept out of their reach. Ensure electric cables or anything that could be a risk are covered or out of the way. Offer lots of dog toys that are designed to be chewed and are safe.

It is important that you don't over exercise until they are fully formed. Instead offer lots of mental stimulation in the form of games indoors.

Encourage them to take their meals in food toys as this will slow their eating and offer them additional enrichment. This should be supervised.

Y is for Young

A young dog is called a puppy and puppies like to chew

Don't tell him off, this is normal, give him something else to do

Pick up your stuff and give him a toy or he might decide he likes your shoe.

Did you know:

If you've never experienced them before, the zoomies are a sudden burst of energy by a dog. They appear on the surface to be going crazy; charging up and down and around and around, but don't worry this is not uncommon. It is normally a sign of pent up excitement that something has triggered. It might be your arrival home from being out, or it might also be a sign of built up stress.

Things to be aware of are: can the dog injure itself on slippery floors for example or fall down the stairs? If so, open the back door and encourage them into the garden. If you're in the park you're probably fine but be aware of roads.

Z is for Zoomies

Zz

When I get really excited and can't control my feelings

I might zoom around and around so fast

I make you dizzy and start reeling.

With thanks to my wife Felicity, for her constant love, support and encouragement in everything I try to do. I can never repay you, but I will try.

For Megan, the best daughter a father could ever wish for.

For Mum and Dad for always being there, for Jason for being a better brother than I am.

...and for Roxy, my inspiration and the best dog in the world.

Love you all

xXx

Printed in Great Britain
by Amazon